THE
LEGAL
ENGLISH
WORKBOOK

Michael Davies

LEGAL ENGLISH UK
London

www.legalenglish.co.uk

Acknowledgements

The author would like to thank the following for their help with the book:

Students and Teachers of Legal English UK
Christopher J Mitchell
James Lavelle
John Morgan-Davies
Natalie Arsenow

CONTENTS

1. LEGAL WRITING SKILLS

Legal Writing Skills

The English language features many words that share similar definitions. This makes it easy to unknowingly construct a sentence using complex words that are old-fashioned or do not fit. Look at the following example of a police statement which is written in archaic English.

I was proceeding along the main thoroughfare in the panda vehicle when a caucasian male ran out of the antiques emporium.

If we wished to make this more palatable for the reader, we could change it quite easily:

I was driving along the main road in the police car when a white male ran out of the antiques shop.

English can feature many words in a sentence that are not essential. It is very easy for writers to confuse the reader by showing off their linguistic acumen.

It is not necessary for a solicitor to be present in all instances, but we would hope that a legal representative of some level is at least informed if a client is taken into custody.

The sentence can be shortened by avoiding unnecessary expressions and words, making the sentence more direct and adding more appropriate verbs. For example, it could be turned into a conditional sentence.

"If our client is taken into custody, a legal representative should be contacted."

Try and resist the need to 'show off' in Legal English. Use the right words and write clearly. Keep sentences to a maximum of 20 words if possible. Write short paragraphs that do not annoy the reader.

Exercise One
Using Modern English

The following sentences have been written in old-fashioned English. Write them in a more modern way.

1) Pursuant to the terms of the aforementioned document, we suggest that you vacate the premises with immediate effect.

....

....

2) We write with reference to the above-mentioned dwelling.

....

....

3) We think it fair to say that the resolvement of the case depends upon the judicial stigmatism of the court deciding it.

....

....

4) Upon hearing about the way that the defence had conducted the case, the court decided that it was wise to look again at the opprobrium that had been caused by the Netflix documentary.

....

....

5) The aforementioned parties were unaware of the mischief that had been caused.

....

....

6) Henceforth, any defendant who wishes to address the court must do so through counsel.

....

....

7) Enclosed herewith you will find a copy of my curriculum vitae.

....

....

Exercise Two
Using strong verbs

Legal English writers rely heavily on the use of the *to be* verb in their writing when a normal verb would be far better for the reader. The following sentences are written with the *to be* verb. All you have to do is replace each of them with a more dynamic verb where possible.

1) The Judge was of the opinion that the claimant was not able to provide sufficient evidence.

....

....

....

2) There is no express term in the contract to suggest that the package should have been delivered to Mark Knox.

....

....

3) The barrister is in direct disagreement with the Judge on this matter.

....

....

4) Four people are accused of committing numerous acts of fraud against the Nary Investment Bank.

....

....

5) As there are several people involved in the claim, I would suggest that we try and use one solicitor.

....

....

6) The indications are that the other side is in a position to settle for a not insubstantial sum.

....

....

Exercise Three
Legal letter writing

As a successful lawyer, your working day will be filled with many responsibilities. When you're not meeting clients, you're on the telephone with them or attending court. Regrettably, few lawyers take the time to draft high quality letters. Clients pay a lot of attention to legal correspondence and it is worth taking a few extra minutes to write professionally. Here are some snippets of advice on how to write a great letter.

Know your audience
A letter to a corporate client will differ from that to a private client so you should adjust your language accordingly.

Have a strong structure
Just as with a great story, a great letter will have a beginning, a middle and an end.

Keep it real
Avoid unnecessary expressions such as 'it is noted', 'it should be considered' and 'please be aware that'. Nobody talks like this anymore and nobody should write like it either.

Reduce your errors

One former colleague of mine used to drive legal secretaries crazy with his demands for perfect grammar and spelling but it made sense because that letter reflected on him and the firm he worked for - and he wanted it to be perfect.

Address your letter correctly

There are different ways to begin and end a letter depending on the recipient. If you know the name of the person (Dear Mr Jones, Dear Susan) then you should end the letter with *Yours sincerely*. If you do not know the name of the person (Dear Sirs, Dear Sir/Madam) then you should end your letter with *Yours faithfully*.

Writing a letter

The letter below is too informal. Rewrite it so that it is clearer, more formal and in plain English. There are also some spelling errors which you should correct.

Dear Kevin

I am glad that you were up for a visit to my office today, particularly considering you had been feeling a little worse for wear after a heavy night.

You told me that you had been sacked by your employer for steeling stationery and that you were not guilty of this allegation. There was no proof that you did it and even if there was, the value of the items that you allegedly stole were so ridiculously low that your employer should have forgotten about it anyway.

I think that we should write a letter to your farmer boss asking him what the deal is. If he comes back with the same old nonsense that he told you before then we should sue him.

In the unlikely event that his response is more positive then you can consider your options.

If you would like to have a chinwag, just pick up the phone and give me a holler.

....

....

....

....

....

....

....

....

....

....

....

....

....

....

....

....

Exercise Four
Passive Voice

The active voice is more effective than the passive voice as it is clearer, shorter and more direct. The passive voice usually hides crucial information and places emphasis on the wrong place. It should be avoided wherever possible.

Active voice sentences follow this format:
Subject - Verb - Object

Passive voice sentences following this format:
Object - verb - subject

Change the following sentences from passive voice to active voice:

1. The defendant was found not guilty by a majority verdict.

   ....

   ....

2. I felt that the Judge was determined to rule that the evidence was inadmissable.

....

....

....

3. Our side is of the opinion that compensation of under £50,000 is completely unacceptable.

....

....

....

4. It was proposed that our client accept the other side's offer.

....

....

....

5. The judgment was delivered to great silence by the majority of the courtroom yet one or two continued to talk.

....

....

6. The protestor was removed from the courtroom by the bailiff and was charged with contempt of court.

....

....

7. The victim was murdered by the defendant with a shotgun.

....

....

8. There was a feeling among defence counsel that their client could have received a lighter sentence.

....

Exercise Five
Letter writing skills
The contents of the letter below have been mixed up.
Put the sections into the correct order.

(a)
Marvin Jones
22 Cherry Blossom Road
Wavertree
London

(b)
Once this has been done and the seller has answered
specific questions regarding the condition of the property
we should be able to complete the purchase within four
to six weeks.

(c)
Thank you for taking the time to visit our office on 29
May.

(d)
3 June 20XX

(e)
John Poindexter
Poindexter and Mann Solicitors

(f)
During the meeting, you informed me that you have had an offer accepted on the above property and that you would like us to act on your behalf in its purchase.

(g)
If you have any questions, please do not hesitate to contact me at the email address above.

(h)
Purchase of 28 Bloomer Road

(i)
I am now in the process of conducting various searches relating to the property and will also be contacting The Land Registry to clarify the title.

(j)
Ref: POI/JON/2437

(k)
Dear Mr Jones

(l)
Yours sincerely

1) .... 2) .... 3) .... 4) .... 5) ....

6) .... 7) .... 8) .... 9) .... 10) ....

11) .... 12)............

Exercise Six
Replacing nouns with verbs
While you should keep your writing interesting by using a mixture of linguistic devices, you should restrict the use of nouns as often as you can. Use strong verbs where possible.

Example
The court made the decision that...
The court decided that...

1) She brought forth the argument that . . .

....

2) He made the choice of a trainee solicitor rather than an associate.

....

3) The man offered the admission that he had stolen the wallet.

....

4) The translator made an interpretation of the affidavit.

....

5) The doctor made a referral of the defendant to a psychiatrist.

....

6) The parties made an agreement that they would not compete in each other's territories.

....

Exercise Seven
Punctuation
When we speak we naturally pause at different moments. Punctuation helps us to do that in writing.

Sentences are made up of clauses. A complete sentence might contain one or several independent clauses with a subject and verb. A dependent clause would require an additional clause to help.

Commas can be used to join two independent clauses with a conjunction such as but or so and after an introductory phrase (however, by doing this, etc.). You can also use them to separate additional information in a sentence (John, who was 24, died last night).

Semicolons are used when joining two independent clauses of equal value.

"The lawyer was a competent litigator; she had won every case since the beginning of the year."

Use the colon to emphasise the second clause in a sentence.

"He had two dogs: Jasper and Rex."

Punctuate the following paragraphs. Add full stops, capitalisation, semicolons, colons and commas where appropriate.

1) chris is one of the most relaxed people i know he is tall and slim with black hair and he always wears a dark jacket and blue jeans his jeans have holes in them and his trainers are scruffy too he usually sits at the back of the lecture hall and he often seems to be asleep however when the exam results are given out he always gets an "A" i don't think hes as lazy as he appears to be

2) the woman wandered into the area and claimed to know the man in charge but he said that he had never met her before in his life which was not what she wanted to hear so she started shouting and screaming and punching and kicking people until the police came and arrested her when she went to the police station her solicitor had a word with the

police and told them that she was under a lot of stress so they let her off with a warning

3) your claim for damages is likely to be considered seriously by the court but you should note that there are several mitigating factors which they may bring into consideration and which is beyond our control and even if we had a chance to change the narrative it is only a small chance that is very unlikely to sway the court

4) the court clerks instructed the twelve members of the jury not to speak about the case outside the courtroom the clerks want to protect jury integrity and there were concerns about media interest in the case

5) While the witness maintained a relaxed demeanour through the cross-examination there was

something about her answers that didnt ring true

and i felt that the jury picked up on this

Exercise Eight

Look at the following sentences. Edit them and replace unnecessary words; make each sentence shorter and more direct.

1) While an offer for the company is on the table from one bidder, there is unlikely to be another offer until they clarify the situation.

....

....

....

2) The Judge invited the jury to consider their verdict as to whether the defendant was guilty or not guilty.

....

....

3) Government officials were warned about accepting hospitality and were told that they could as long as it had been permitted under applicable government ethics rules.

....

....

....

4) The basis on which you seek to explain your legal volte face is entirely disingenuous.

....

....

5) Our client has been forced to take legal advice on account of these fundamental procedural flaws which call into question the legitimacy of this investigation.

....

....

6) The council sent a team to investigate the condition of the commercial premises and they promptly issued a closure order under The Anti-Social Behaviour, Crime and Policing Act 2014.

....

....

....

Exercise Nine

Avoiding negative statements

It is too easy in legal writing to resort to negative words and phrases for the sake of attempting to make your writing more formal. You should avoid this where possible and seek to write positive statements. As with many areas of English, there are exceptions to this rule where a negative sentence is unavoidable (no smoking allowed).

Turn the following sentences from negative to positive and make them more direct if possible. The meaning should be kept the same.

1) No more than seven persons are to be allowed in this room at any one time.

....

....

2) In the unlikely event that the witness is not available, please do not attempt to contact him unless we tell you to do so.

....

....

3) It is an unarguable statement that the gentleman I represent did not commit the crime that he has been accused of.

....

....

4) This can not be construed as an admission of guilt by my client.

....

....

5) He should not interpret this as a breach of contract but rather as a haphazard attempt to revise an agreement that he considered unworkable.

....

....

2. THE LEGAL PROFESSION

The Legal Profession

There are two branches of the legal profession in England and Wales - barristers and solicitors.

Barristers are the lawyers that you are probably most familiar with; we usually see them in films or television dramas. They prosecute and defend cases in higher courts and are skilled in litigation.

In appearances at some courts (although notably not The Supreme Court) they wear wigs and gowns.

People come into contact more often with solicitors. If you buy a house, commit a crime, write a will, lose your job or start a company then you will need a solicitor at some point in the process.

Solicitors are easy to find. If you walk down any high street in any city or town in the UK then you will find a solicitors' firm with solicitors ready to act on your behalf.

To become a solicitor, you will typically have taken a three-year degree course in law at university and followed this with a one-year Legal Practice Course (although this will change to the SQE soon). A two-year traineeship follows where you spend time in four different departments within a law firm shadowing senior solicitors and doing minor casework.

Barristers are more difficult to find as an individual usually needs to be introduced to one by a solicitor with the solicitor acting as an intermediary.

In London, barristers are usually based at one of the four Inns of Court. These are verdant little villages within London that might seem out of place compared with the hustle and bustle of the city.

Barristers take their own professional course known as the Bar Practice Course before starting a pupillage within 'Chambers'. Chambers is an office consisting of many different barristers which can be found at the Inns of Court or at cities across England and Wales. Barristers are typically self-employed and take cases on the 'cab rank principle'. This means that the next barrister on the list takes the next case and so on.

A senior barrister is known as a QC or Queen's Counsel. They are also known as silks because of the material of their gowns as worn in the courtroom.

Exercise One

Key Words

Fill in the gaps using these keywords from the text. Remember to use the correct tense.

Commit	Solicitor	Barrister	Pupillage
Chambers	Silk	Traineeship	Will

1. She definitely needs a .... if she wants to draw up that kind of agreement.

2. After trying for several years, Ursula finally managed to take ....

3. He joined .... at the start of the year as a pupil.

4. The .... has been located and is with the solicitor now. It is only two pages long so will be read quickly.

5. He applied for a .... at the law firm and is hoping for a positive response.

6. Before joining the Chambers, he had a .... with Royston Doyston QC.

7. The story was that she .... the murder in cold blood.

8. After becoming a ...., he chose to specialise in tax law.

Exercise Two

The Language of the Courtroom

This is a sketch of the criminal court – known in England and Wales as the Crown Court. Try and identify as many of the numbers as you can.

1 ...., 2.............., 3..............., 4..............., 5...............,

6............., 7.............., 8................., 9.............., 10.............,

11..........., 12............, 13.............., 14............, 15...............,

16..........., 17............., 18.............., 19............., 20.............. ..

Exercise Three

Fill in the missing words in this article about the UK Supreme Court.

Hear   Separation   Responsibilities

Appeal   Leads   Ruling

The Supreme Court of the United Kingdom

While the UK has one of the oldest legal systems in the world, its Supreme Court is one of the youngest courts of last resort. It began its work in 2009, taking over (a) …………………. from the judicial branch of the House of Lords. The government of the day felt that there needed to be a greater (b) ………………….. of powers between the judiciary and the legislature and so The Supreme Court was born.

There are 12 justices in total, although it is rare for them to all (c) ……….. a case at the same time.

Recent cases of The UK Supreme Court include the well-known 'Brexit case' R (Miller) v Secretary of State for Exiting the European Union and a (d) …….……….. on excessive fees introduced by the government on bringing claims for unfair dismissal.

The Supreme Court justices also sit on the Judicial Committee of the Privy Council. Some commonwealth countries still use this committee as their final e) ….……….... court which f) …..……….. to the occasional situation where judges in London have to decide on cases involving the death penalty, which is still carried out in Trinidad for example but has not been used in the UK since the 1960s.

Exercise 4

1. How many justices are on The UK Supreme Court?

   ……………………………………………………………………………….

2. When did The Supreme Court first open its doors?

   ……………………………………………………………………………….

3. Which court did The Supreme Court replace?

....

How to compare in Legal English

There are several different ways to compare in English. The most common is through comparatives and superlatives. This table explains how to use them.

Adjective form	Comparative	Superlative
Only one syllable, ending in E. Examples: *wide, fine, cute*	Add -R: *wider, finer, cuter*	Add -ST: *widest, finest, cutest*
Only one syllable, with one vowel and one consonant at the end. Examples: *hot, big, fat*	Double the consonant, and add -ER: *hotter, bigger, fatter*	Double the consonant, and add -EST: *hottest, biggest, fattest*
Only one syllable, with more than one vowel or more than one consonant at the end. Examples: *light, neat, fast*	Add -ER: *lighter, neater, faster*	Add -EST: *lightest, neatest, fastest*
Two syllables, ending in Y. Examples: *happy, silly, lonely*	Change Y to I, then add -ER: *happier, sillier, lonelier*	Change Y to I, then add -EST: *happiest, silliest, loneliest*
Two syllables or more, not ending in Y. Examples: *modern, interesting, beautiful*	Use MORE before the adjective: *more modern, more interesting, more beautiful*	Use MOST before the adjective: *most modern, most interesting, most beautiful*

Another way to compare is through similes. This occurs when one forms an expression using the structure *AS + ADJECTIVE + AS*. There are some examples below:

The UK Supreme Court is not as powerful as The US Supreme Court as Parliament remains sovereign.

The lawyer from Firm A is just as competent as the lawyer from Firm B.

Exercise Five

Try the exercise below to test your knowledge of comparisons.

1. There are four Inns of Court. The ……………………….….… by far is Lincoln's Inn, which covers 11 acres of land.

2. The Supreme Court is the ……………………….. court in the United Kingdom.

3. It has been suggested that contract law is as
   .... a subject as criminal law, maybe
   more so.

4. I still think that the television show Rumpole of the
   Bailey is .... than Suits.

5. Judge Smith is .... than
   Judge Jones. It is very difficult to get a positive
   decision from him.

6. It's sometimes .... to admit that you're
   guilty and take a deal than risk a court hearing.

Exercise Six

Legal Phrasal Verbs

While phrasal verbs occur more frequently in informal
spoken English, an international lawyer with a strong
command of English should be able to use phrasal
verbs in legal documents with the same natural ease as
a native speaker. For this exercise, try and link the
phrasal verbs with the definition.

Take over	Follow
Look over	Discard
Serve upon	Deliver
Adhere to	Save
Bail out	Read quickly
Rule out	Take control

Exercise Seven

Add the appropriate phrasal verb to each sentence. Make sure that you use the appropriate tense. There is one phrasal verb that is not required.

1. The client's solicitors have agreed to
   ..…………………………………………………….the plan in
   order to present a united front to their client.

2. The lawyer told the court that the document had
   been…………………………….the plaintiff last week.

3. Two banks were …………………………………..by the
   government to the tune of several billion pounds.

4. The Judge..the statement before it was read to the court.

5. Steven Jones has......................................the case and will be in charge from now on.

Legal English Vocabulary: Doublets

As the English language has evolved, it has taken words from a myriad of other languages. This is why one frequently finds six or seven words of similar meaning. Legal English uses many doublets, particularly in contracts. One reason for this is so that the contract can be considered unambiguous, although doublets can also appear confusing to the non-lawyer.

Fit and Proper = Trustworthy

The Premier League has instigated a Fit and Proper Person test to ensure that all new Chairmen are competent and trustworthy.

Null and Void = Void

The court declared the contract to be null and void due to the breach made by the first party.

Over and Above = More than is necessary

He promised to go over and above the terms of his contract when he joined the firm.

Part and Parcel = Part

The 85-year-old partner is part and parcel of the firm and cannot be asked to leave.

Good and Chattels = Goods

The will states that all goods and chattels will be passed to the beneficiary.

Terms and Conditions = The details of a contract

Take a look at the Terms and Conditions and check if you agree with everything.

Exercise Eight

Fit one of the doublets mentioned above into the following sentences:

1. Nigel Markesby has failed his ………………………………………………. test and will no longer be allowed to take over as Chairman of Roichester Rovers.

2. The contract was declared …..……………………….. by the court.

3. Being a good draughtsman is ………….……………… of being a lawyer.

Exercise Nine

Informal to formal

These extracts have been written too informally. Can you rewrite them to make them more formal?

1. Your lawyer is Miss Nash.

   ....

2. The sale of your house will probably take place on 30 June.

   ....

   ....

3. You can have a training contract from us if you want it.

   ....

   ....

4. The court thought that the criminal committed the crime.

   ....

   ....

5. The US Supreme Court has nine judges but the UK Supreme Court has 12.

   ....

   ....

6. The training contract is two years and lawyers usually do four different departments.

   ....

   ....

Exercise Ten

Match these legal words with their more general English alternatives.

Heretofore   It stands

Affidavit   Property that can be inherited

Bailiff   Witness statement

Stare Decisis   Debt collector

Hereditament   Before

3. COMPANY LAW

Company Law

It is easy to start a business in the UK, particularly if you run it as a sole trader or a partnership.

Both of these types of company have unlimited liability. This means that the owners are obligated to cover any debts that the company incurs.

The alternative is to set up a company that has limited liability, meaning that investors are protected if the company incurs debt that it cannot pay.

If you intend to run a company with limited liability, you will need to register the business at Companies House in Cardiff. You will need to place at least two documents with them: the Memorandum of Association and the Articles of Association.

The Memorandum is a legal statement agreeing to form a company while the Articles are the rules connected with the running of the company.

You must also send your annual accounts and details of any changes to Companies House.

In the box below, you will find the various types of companies that you can set up in the UK.

Sole Trader	Partnership	Limited Liability Partnership (LLP)
Public Limited Company (PLC)	Limited company (Ltd.)	

Exercise One
Which type of business possesses the following characteristics?

1. Owned by and run by its members

   ....

2. These companies must be registered at Companies House.

   ....

3. Owners receive dividends from profits based on their shareholding

   ....

4. Firms requiring little investment are usually these type

....

5. Investors have limited liability

....

6. These organisations need at least two partners.

....

7. There must be an annual audit of this type of business without any exceptions.

....

8. There is a separate legal persona distinct from its owners.

....

9. Capital is provided by the partners.

....

Exercise Two
Salomon v Salomon
Read the essay and fill in the missing words.

distinguish   independent   sole

unlimited   creditors

Salomon v Salomon is a landmark case in company law as it established the principle of a company having a 'separate legal persona' distinct from its shareholders.

Aaron Salomon was a boot maker in Whitechapel in East London. The business had originally been run as a (1) .... trader - so Mr Salomon had (2) .... liability for the debts of the company. Salomon then transferred it into a limited company with shares owned by members of his family. The business went into liquidation and (3) .... sought to recover debts owed.

The liquidator, acting on behalf of the creditors, alleged that the limited company was merely an agent of Mr Salomon and that he should be personally liable for the debt. In other words, there was no separate legal persona to (4) .... Salomon Ltd. from Mr Salomon.

The Court of Appeal ruled that the limited company was a myth and had been created purely to protect Mr Salomon. However, the House of Lords, which was then the final appeal court, reversed the decision of the Court of Appeal and ruled that it was completely (5) .... of its shareholders and with its own rights and responsibilities.

Exercise Three

Letter of Advice

The paragraphs in the following letter have been mixed up. Put them into the correct order.

You explained that you wish to open a coffee shop and have identified the premises and begun the process of sourcing suppliers and finding staff. You plan to inject capital of £75,000 into the business which is partly from your own funds as well as investments from friends and family.   (a)

Thank you for taking the time to meet with me at our office last Friday where we discussed your options for starting a new company.   (b)

Once you have considered my advice, please do not hesitate to contact me as I will be delighted to assist you in filing the paperwork for this.   (c)

As a coffee shop is a somewhat risky venture and you will have several investors, I suggest that you form a limited company. There are many advantages to such a move including the limited liability you and any fellow shareholders will face if something goes wrong, significant tax incentives and much easier access to finance should you wish to build the company. Suppliers are far keener to deal with limited companies than sole traders. (d)

You told me that you wish to start a business and were seeking advice as to what form it should take. I explained that there are several options open to you, particularly setting up a limited company or as a sole trader. (e)

Place the paragraphs into their correct order.

1…………... 2…………... 3…………... 4…………... 5…………...

Exercise Four
   1. What type of business does the client wish to start?

    …………………………………………………………………………..

   2. Why did the solicitor recommend that her client form a limited company?

    …………………………………………………………………………

    …………………………………………………………………………..

3. What does 'risky' mean?

....

....

Exercise Five
Odd Word Out
Circle the odd word out in each group of words.

1. Establish   Found   Liquidate   Start up

2. Rival   Acquaintance   Competitor
   Challenger

3. Colleague   Co-worker   Associate   Antagonist

4. Board   Executive   Department   Top brass

5. Go public   IPO   Share offer   Rights issue

6. Merger   Spin-off   Amalgamation
   Confederation

Sole Trader
If your business is low risk and requires little initial
investment, operating as a sole trader can be a viable
option. You simply start your business. It does not
involve any registration fees and the only authority you
will need to register with is Her Majesty's Revenue and

Customs (HMRC) for tax purposes.

The main disadvantage is that you are responsible for any debts that your business incurs. If your business gets into serious amounts of debt, you risk losing personal assets to repay the debts.

The primary legal obligation you have is to send a self-assessment form each year to HMRC detailing your profits for the year. This has to be done by a particular deadline or you risk having to pay a fine.

Exercise Six
1. What does HMRC mean and what do they do?

    ....

    ....

2. What is unlimited liability?

    ....

    ....

3. Why would an entrepreneur prefer to be a sole trader?

....

....

Exercise Seven
Questions and Answers

Link the question and answers.

1. What did you do at Companies House?

2. What does your business do?

3. What are your obligations as a limited company?

4. Why did you change to a limited company?

5. How is business?

A
"I run a small business which sells t-shirts with slogans and cartoons on them."

B
"Initially, I ran it as a sole trader but as I wanted to grow the business and find premises I decided to form a limited company."

C
"The first few years were tough because of the level of

competition and nobody knew who we were. I took advice from professionals and worked hard on my social media presence. After about 18 months, we were starting to break even and by the third year we were looking at expanding."

D
"Quite a lot actually. We had to register the business at Companies House and have to file paperwork every year and when there is a substantial change in the business."

E
"We had to register a Charge because we borrowed some money from the bank to grow the business."

Exercise Eight
Prepositions

1. He resolved ………………. make a decision on the future of the company over the weekend.

2. This decision is ……….. the discretion ………….. the Company Secretary.

3. We write in response ………………. your earlier letter.

4. The relationship ………………. management and

trade unions has changed dramatically in the last 30 years.

5. The AGM is likely to vote ……………. the executive pay package next month.

6. He decided to set ………………… a business when he was made redundant.

7. An LLP is similar in many ways ………………… a partnership.

Exercise Nine
Vocabulary
Unjumble the letters so that they make sense.

1. To set up and register a new company. (REOPTAIOCNR)

2. Share of the profits of a company paid to shareholders. (VDEIDNDI)

3. Maximum amount of share capital for a company to have. (OEDAUIHSRT)

4. The owner is completely responsible for the business. (BITLILIYA)

5. A partner who contributes money but who does not participate in the business. (ELGSPNIE)

1 …......…..............................……......…

2 …......…..............................……......…

3 …......…...............................……......…

4….......…...............................……......…

5 …......…...............................……......…

Partnership Agreement
A partnership agreement sets out the details of relationships between the parties. Read through the example agreement and answer the questions that follow.

OBLIGATIONS OF PARTNERS

Each Partner agrees at all times:

to use his best skills and endeavours towards the successful operating of the Partnership and at all times conduct himself in a fair and proper manner in all transactions of any nature affecting the Partnership;

to disclose to the other Partners any matter that may prejudice the business prospects of the Partnership and generally show the utmost good faith to the other Partners in all transactions relating to the Partnership;

not to disclose Confidential Information to any person, firm or business unless with the prior written consent of all the other Partners;

that no other partners will be added to the Partnership without the express prior written approval of all of the Partners;

to keep proper records of all business transacted by or on behalf of the Partnership;

to duly and punctually pay and discharge his separate and private debts and liabilities and keep the Partnership, the Partnership Property and the other Partners and their respective estates and effects indemnified against all actions, proceedings, costs, claims, and demands in relation to such private debts and liabilities;

to comply with all regulations, professional standards and other provisions about the conduct of the Partnership's business generally, including any directions made from time to time by the Partners.

Exercise Ten

1) Formal word meaning to follow

....

2) What is a fiduciary duty?

....

3) What is your understanding of 'to keep proper records'?

....

4) What does discharge mean?

....

Exercise 11
AGMs and EGMs

There are two types of meetings which public limited companies are obliged to call: AGMs and EGMs.

The annual general meeting (AGM) is an opportunity for shareholders to question directors and vote on issues relating to the company. While retail investors (private individuals) can attend and vote, they have very little influence in comparison with institutional investors such as pension funds and investment trusts.

A public limited company must hold its AGM within six months of the end of the financial year. The board of directors will decide where the AGM takes place but it should try and do so in a place that has convenient access for shareholders. A private company no longer needs to hold an AGM unless specified in the articles of association.

At the AGM, shareholders will hear about the progress of the company and have the chance to vote on the appointment of directors and auditors as well as consider the company accounts (shareholders are not able to vote on the accounts – just consider them).

An extraordinary general meeting (EGM) is held to consider emergency matters that cannot wait for the AGM. Some examples include the removal of a director or a significant legal matter.

The power to call an EGM is laid out in the Companies Act 2013 which allows shareholders who own at least 10% of shares to demand a meeting. If the directors agree then the meeting may be held. If they disagree then it can be for a court to decide.

1. What is the difference between an AGM and an EGM?

   ....

   ....

2. Which statute sets out the rules for calling an EGM?

   ....

3. What is meant by 'a show of hands'?

   ....

Public Limited Companies

A public limited company (PLC) trades on the stock exchange. In the UK, the main share index is the FTSE 100 which is made up of the 100 biggest companies by value. It includes companies worth billions of pounds such as Vodafone and British Airways.

There are other share indexes such as the FTSE 250 and the FTSE 350. The AIM share index is a list of smaller companies worth several million pounds.

Exercise 12

Match the words with their definitions.

Commission   Index fund Broker   Market maker

Ex-dividend   Go public   Offer   Stamp duty

1. If you buy shares in the company after this date then you will not receive a share of the profits.

   ....

2. A collection of shares linked to the FTSE 100 (for example) which people can invest in.

   ....

3. An intermediary who buys and sells shares on your behalf.

   ....

4. The colloquial expression used when a company is in the process of becoming a public limited company.

   ....

5. This is usually a bank or financial institution that acts as a wholesaler for shares.

   ....

6. The tax charged on shares.

   ………………………………………...

7. A percentage fee charged by a professional.

   ………………………………………....

8. The opportunity to buy shares. Also known as an IPO.

   ………………………………………....

Exercise 13
Informal to formal
On the left are less formal versions of words used in corporate law. Match them with the more formal expressions on the right side.

Research	Write down
Confirm	Deliver
Ship	Authenticate
Accept	Acknowledge
Get	Obtain
Owner	Reconnaissance

Record   Cite

Mention   Principal

Exercise 14
Crossword
Look at the clues below and find the answers in the crossword.

J	K	A	C	Q	U	I	R	E	X
O	D	I	V	I	D	E	N	D	K
I	E	D	K	H	Y	F	J	H	L
N	B	W	S	P	L	I	T	O	F
T	E	G	I	L	P	O	R	S	N
K	N	U	M	A	S	S	E	T	H
J	T	A	R	G	E	T	B	I	T
V	U	K	L	O	F	Q	L	L	P
F	R	A	N	C	H	I	S	E	O
Z	E	J	P	R	S	O	F	J	Z

1) Purchase a company.

2) An unsecured bond designed to raise money for a business or government.

3) This business sells the products of a larger company and pays a fee.

4) An unwelcome act.

5) Abbreviation for an entity which allows for protection of each partner's financial liabilities.

6) A division of shares to make them more marketable for retail investors.

7) A company that may be subject to takeover by another company.

8) Fill in the missing word: ……… and several.

9) Something of value to a business

10) Money paid twice a year to shareholders

Exercise 15
What type of business?
The following clients have come to you for advice as to what type of business to set up. Read their comments and suggest which business is preferable and why.

1. I have started selling a few items on eBay and Amazon. It's mostly books and objects that I find lying around the house. I am worried about tax implications if the business takes off and is really

successful.

....

2. I am setting up an accountancy firm with some colleagues and I wonder if we should consider a partnership or an LLP. What are your thoughts on the subject?

....

....

....

3. I am buying a commercial premises in the centre of town and I want to open a shop selling clothes and knick-knacks. How do I limit my risks?

....

....

....

4. I'm going to work for Uber and was wondering whether I should set myself up as a limited company or not?

....

Exercise 16
Match Game
Match the services with the client's requirements.

Articles of association   M & A law

Partnership agreement   Negotiation

Memorandum of association

1. Clients have visited your office to sign a document confirming that their company has officially started.

   ....

2. The clients are discussing which rules are needed regarding the running of the company.

   ....

3. Your client is selling a franchise to a new franchisee.

....

....

4. This document needs to include provisions as to what happens in the event of the death of a member.

....

5. The client is considering buying a smaller rival.

....

4. Contract Law

Steve Jones is a contract law solicitor who has been asked to speak to a group of businessmen and women about the essential elements of contract law. Part of his speech is below but some words are missing. Add an appropriate word.

Exercise One

The equation taught to law students who 1) ……………… contract law is one that you must commit to memory: offer + acceptance + consideration = contract. This means that a contract is 2) ………………… only when an offer by one party known as the offeror is accepted by the second party known as the 3) ………….. Consideration is the value exchanged between the parties. Crucially, it has to be sufficient in the eyes of the law.

In addition to that equation, we know that there has to be serious 4) …………………….. on the part of both parties to create a legal relationship so a handshake between friends over something trivial would not be considered a contract. Parties also have to have legal 5) ………..………..., meaning that they are over the age of 18 and are of sufficiently sound mind to understand what's going on.

Let's say that Joe puts an advert on a website for a painting for sale at £50. Steven sees the advertisement and emails Joe with a 6) …………..……….. of £40. Joe counters with £45 and the deal is then done. You have all the elements of a contract in that brief email exchange just as you would in a complex negotiation over trade, for example.

Exercise Two

Unilateral	Duress	Legal capacity	Privity
Consideration	Implied	Bilateral	Express
Invitation to Treat	Boilerplate	Undue influence	Mistake

1. There are two types of contract. What are they?

   ………………………………………………………………………….

2. Under what circumstances can a contract be cancelled?

   …………………………………………………………………………..

3. Force Majeure and Entire Agreement are examples of what type of clause?

   ....

4. Aside from offer and acceptance, what else do the parties need to form a contract?

   ....

5. What is the word used in English law to indicate that negotiation is possible?

   ....

6. What doctrine or rule covers third party rights in a contract?

   ....

Exercise Three
Link these conversations together

1. Is the contract valid if I signed it while I was drunk?	a. It's an express term. Most unusual. Make sure you point it out to the tenant before he signs it.
2. There's a reward of £50 for a missing cat. Do they have to pay me if I find it?	b. Yes, but it's obviously an implied term so it doesn't matter if it is in the contract or not.
3. There is something odd in this Tenancy Agreement that I've not seen in previous ones. Can you check it for me?	c. Yes, there might be some issues regarding consideration as the value is far above that.
4. I can't believe she is only paying £200,000 for that house.	d. Yes, he could claim for breach of contract as a result of a mistake.
5. Are there any boilerplate clauses missing from this contract?	e. The courts would probably consider it to be undue influence and therefore not valid.
6. He's been doing a second job for two months and said that there was nothing in the	f. Yes, you can sue the drinks manufacturer even though you didn't pay for the drink yourself.

contract to stop him.	
7. Does it matter if we deliver a blue car rather than a red car?	g. Yes, the bilateral agreement will be signed next week at The White House.
8. That's crazy! This website has a flat screen TV for sale for £20! I'm buying ten!	h. Yes, it is a unilateral contract and so you can consider it to be an offer to the whole world.
9. The peace deal between Monrovia and the United States took a long time to agree.	I. You will need to add a force majeure clause towards the end.
10. Who can I sue if my friend bought me a drink and I found a slug in it?	j. Sorry to burst your bubble but it's an invitation to treat. They won't be deemed to have accepted the offer until they send them to you.

1) ...., 2) ...., 3) ...., 4) ....

5) ...., 6) ...., 7) ...., 8) ....

9) ...., 10) ....

Exercise Four
Intention to create legal relations

Sam loves his girlfriend so much that he wants to take her on holiday somewhere beautiful. He picks a great hotel in The Maldives, tells his girlfriend Nancy and she accepts his kind offer gladly. Unfortunately, the fickle finger of fate intervenes and Nancy finds a more interesting boyfriend. Sam tells her that she should pay him back half of the money or ditch her new boyfriend and return to him. She declines.

Questions to ponder.

1) Was there an offer?

    ....

    ....

2) Was there acceptance?

    ....

    ....

3) Was there consideration?

    ....

    ....

4) Was there an intention to create legal relations?

....

....

Case law

Parliament is the supreme legislator, but from the moment Parliament has uttered its will as lawgiver, that will becomes subject to the interpretation put upon it by the judges of the land.
A V Dicey, Constitutional Expert

In England and Wales, case law has a great deal of influence on law. Judges interpret statutes as best they can but it is incorrect to say that judges make the law. All they can do is look at previous cases and/or acts of Parliament and try to understand how it relates to the case that is in front of them.

One of the most well-known cases is *Carlill v Carbolic Smoke Ball Company (1892)*. It is famous for several reasons and remains one of the first cases that law students learn at universities in the UK.

Carlill v Carbolic Smoke Ball Company (1892)

Carbolic Smoke Ball Company placed this advertisement in a selection of newspapers.

The newspaper advertisement placed by Carbolic (the defendant) stated:-

"£100 reward will be paid by the Carbolic Smoke Ball Company to any person who contracts the influenza after having used the ball three times daily for two weeks according to the printed directions supplied with each ball...

£1000 is deposited with the Alliance Bank, showing our sincerity in the matter."

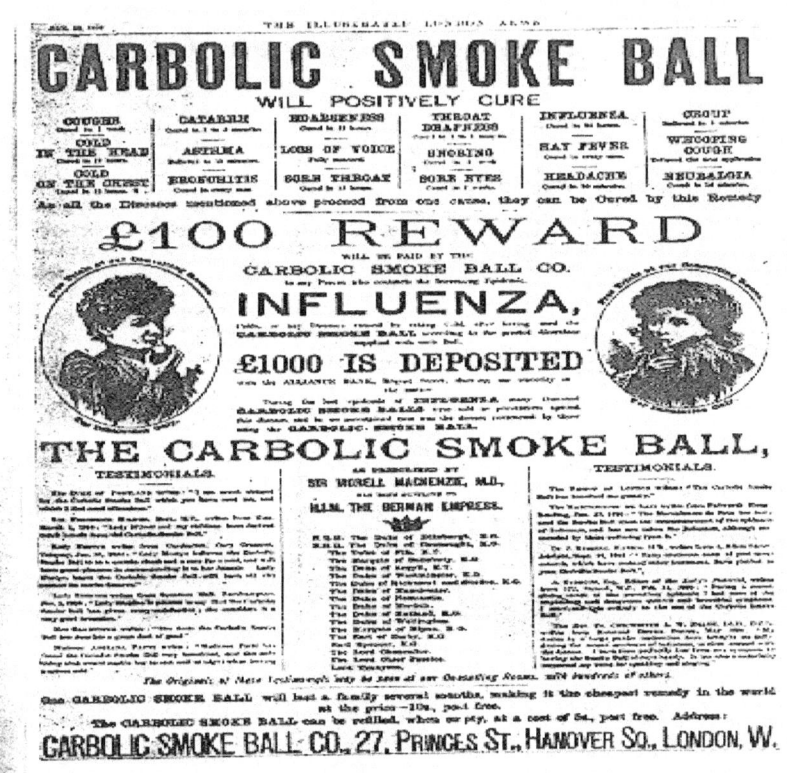

Mrs Carlill (the Claimant) purchased some of these smoke balls and used them according to the directions and promptly caught the flu. She contacted the Carbolic Smoke Ball Company to claim her reward.

One of the questions that the court faced was whether this was a unilateral offer and whether an advertisement could be considered as such or whether it was an invitation to treat. If the court decided it was an invitation to treat then there would have been no contract. This was Carbolic's defence:

1. The advert was a sales puff and lacked intent to be an offer.

2. It is not possible to make an offer to the world.

3. There was no notification of acceptance.

4. The wording was too vague to constitute an offer since there was no stated time limit as to catching the flu.

5. There was no consideration provided since the 'offer' did not specify that the user of the balls must have purchased them.

The Court of Appeal rejected these arguments saying that the advertisement could be considered to be an offer to the select number of people who had read it and who had followed the instructions. They also said that there was consideration as the people buying smoke balls were helping the Carbolic Smoke Ball Company. Additionally, the £1000 that had been deposited in the bank was an indication of intention to create legal relations.

If someone is inviting offers or indicates that they are willing to enter into negotiations but is not prepared to be bound immediately and can accept or reject any offer made – this is called an invitation to treat.

Exercise Five

Here are some situations. Which of these can be construed as offers and which as invitations to treat?

1. Chocolate Bar for Sale - 50p	2. 'I have just bid £25 for those trainers on ebay.'
3. REWARD: £50 to the person who returns my dog.	4. Free holiday to the United States if you buy this £200 TV.
5. Paris Bank invites offers to provide language training courses for its employees.	6. 'Shake my hand and you can have it for £20 right now.'

Offer	Invitation to Treat

Exercise Six
Negotiating

Negotiating is part and parcel of life. Lawyers have to be good negotiators for their clients as livelihoods and lives can depend on their skills. Here are some words and phrases that are connected with negotiation. Can you identify their meaning?

1. Bottom line

a) most important (b) not important (c) the final option

2. Deadlock

(a) a great decision (b) no movement
(c) winning argument

3. Abrasive

(a) friendly   (b) tough   (c) indifferent   (d) intelligent

4. Concede

(a) to lose something   (b) to win something
(c) work with others   (d) compete with others

5. Give and Take

(a) win everything   (b) compromise
(c) steal   (d) borrow

Exercise Seven
Types of Contract Clause

1. Force Majeure	a. Clause that specifies an amount of compensation that the breaching party should pay to the non-breaching party if part of the contract is breached.
2. Payment of Costs	b. Clause detailing which contractual rights, duties and obligations may be assigned to another party.
3. Governing Law	c. One party takes on the responsibility to pay damages for any loss or damage that has been incurred by another individual.
4. Acceleration	d. This clause deals with unforeseen events such as pandemics and wars.
5. Assignment	e. This sets out which nation or state legal system applies in the context of this contract.
6. Liquidated	f. An example of a boilerplate

Damages	clause, this states that everything that you need to know about this contract is in this document and supersedes all other documents and letters.
7. Indemnity	g. This clause states which party is responsible for the payment of costs relating to preparing the agreement.
8. Entire Agreement	h. This clause is frequently found in mortgage or loan contracts and requires the offeree to repay the remainder of their loan immediately if certain requirements have not been met.

Exercise Eight
Contract: Remedies to Breach of Contract

In contract law, a remedy is a resolution ordered by the court to deal with one party's breach of contract and see that justice is done. Breach of contract occurs when one party to a contract has not fulfilled their obligations under the agreement.

The purpose of the remedies below is to place the injured party in the position they would have otherwise been in had the contract been performed as was agreed.

For this exercise, please link the remedies with their definitions.

1. Compensatory Damages	a. If either undue influence, fraud, duress or mistake has occurred then this means that the duties and obligations of both parties are terminated and the contract no longer exists.
2. Punitive Damages	b. This is a rare remedy as it is considered impractical. In this instance, the court requires the contract to be completed.

3. Rescission	c. This is split into pecuniary and non-pecuniary damages and it refers to financial compensation for expenses that can be quantified such as medical costs and things that cannot be quantified such as emotional damage.
4. Specific Performance	d. This remedy returns the injured party to the state they were in prior to the contract being created.
5. Restitution	e. These are also known as exemplary damages and are used to punish the wrongdoer. They are rare in contract law cases but you occasionally see them in tort cases such as defamation.

Exercise Nine
Odd Words Out

Which word on each line is the odd one out?

1) reject   repudiate   sanction   dismiss
2) hold   transfer   assign   transmit
3) provision   clause   codicil   whole
4) boilerplate termination consideration severability
5) deleted   strike out allow   expunge

Exercise Ten

Complete the sentences below.

1. A contract is formed when the ....

   accepts an offer from the ....

2. If a contract has been .... then the

   defendant is entitled to seek ....

3. .... is the usual remedy awarded by

   the courts for breach of contract.

4. The buyer shall give the seller two weeks

   .... of shipment.

5. They have both decided to enter ………………… a contract.

6. He intends to ………………… damages for breach of contract.

Exercise 11
Idioms and Phrasal Verbs
The article contains several idioms and phrasal verbs. Read the article and then find and match the idioms with their definitions below.

One of the most well-known English contract law cases is *Balfour v Balfour*. Mr Balfour had tied the knot with Mrs Balfour and they moved to Sri Lanka for Mr Balfour to take over a civil service post.

They came back to England in 1915 and Mrs Balfour became under the weather. The doctor said that she had come down with rheumatoid arthritis and advised her to stay in England.

Mr Balfour returned to Sri Lanka and told his wife that he would send her a pick-me-up of £30 each month to tide her over until she joined him back in Sri Lanka.

He kept his end of the bargain for a couple of years but unfortunately, the couple were no longer seeing eye-to-eye and drifted apart. Mr Balfour stopped sending the payments to his wife.

Lord Justice Atkin's statement at the Court of Appeal has now formed the basis of a precedent that remains the law today regarding the intention to create legal relations.

He stated that in a case involving a husband and wife, there could be no intention to create a legal contract because it was a purely domestic arrangement.

Half of a deal:

No longer agree:

Ill:

Develop an illness:

Separate:

Get married:

Financial help:

Help out:

Assume control:

Exercise 12

Complete these sentences with idioms or phrasal verbs that you have used above.

1. Gill and Gareth are hoping to ……………………………. in July.

2. She can't come to work today because she is feeling…………………………………………………………………….

3. I am happy to agree to this as long as she keeps to her …………………………………………………………….

4. The CEO and the CFO have ……………………. in recent years and no longer see ………………………………………….

5. She was clearly struggling so Martin sent her a ……………………..……… of £200 to ………………..………………..

5. Employment Law

The Employment Rights Act (ERA) 1996 is the most important legislation on employer/employee relations. It sets out rules on dismissal, parental leave and redundancy. This Act incorporates older statutes that the government felt needed to be updated.

Important parts of the ERA include the right to receive the main terms of your job in writing, protection from being unfairly dismissed and the right to compensation if your job is no longer necessary.

The UK has an hourly minimum wage which is enshrined in law thanks to The Minimum Wage Act 1998.

This means that employers are legally required to pay their employees the statutory minimum wage. The government can initiate legal proceedings against any employer who is not paying the minimum wage.

The Employment Relations Act 1999 deals with trade unions in the workplace.

Throughout the 1980s, Trade Unions were marginalised under the government of Margaret Thatcher so the 1999 Act sought to redress the balance between trade unions and employers. The act gave new rights to workers and introduced new procedures for collective bargaining in the workplace - allowing groups of employees to negotiate over pay and conditions.

There are also laws against discriminating against people on the grounds of race, age, sex, disability and trade union membership.

Exercise One

1. Which act of law deals with trade union relations?

   ....

2. What does 'redress the balance' mean?

   ....

   ....

3. What can the government do if it catches an employer not paying the minimum wage?

   ....

4. What is 'collective bargaining'?

   ....

   ....

Exercise Two
Connect these words to make collocations.

Negotiated	Dismissal
Employment	Rights
Redress	Bargaining
Minimum	Tribunal
Employment	Settlement
Unfair	The Balance
Collective	Wage

Exercise Three

Now place the collocations into the following sentences:

1. The wage deal was agreed after a process of

   ....

2. A local business has been accused of failing to pay

   the .... to several of its employees.

3. Her solicitor told her that she could bring a claim

   for .... against her former

   employer.

4. The government has promised to ....

   between employees in the north and south of the

   country.

5. It was clear that a .... was unlikely so

   the claim went to an ....

A Contract of Employment

In the UK, there is always a contract between employer and employee but it might not always be in writing. By law, your employer must provide a written statement of terms and conditions within two months of you starting work.

These are some of the express terms you are likely to find in a contract of employment.

Salary, overtime pay and bonus payments
Hours of work
Holiday pay and holiday entitlement
Sick pay
Redundancy pay
Notice period
Disciplinary and grievance procedures
Non-compete clauses/restrictive covenants
Governing law

These are implied terms which do not need to be written into the contract.

Duty of trust between employer and employee
Duty of care
Duty to obey reasonable instructions

Exercise Four

Below are several clauses from a contract of employment. Fill in the missing words.

Benefits   Entitled   Statutory   Procedure

Discounted   Raise   Required

Benefits

You'll be 1) …….....…………...…….…. to health insurance,
2) ……………………………………...…..……. gym membership
and use of a company vehicle. Your entitlement to these
3) …………………………………...….……. will start on June 24 20XX.

Notice period

The notice you must give to end your employment is four weeks.

We may end your employment at any time by giving you four weeks or the 4) ……………....…………….. notice you're
5) …………….………… to, whichever is longer.

Grievances

If you wish to 6) …………………..………… a grievance, you should put it in writing to your line manager.

The grievance 7) …………..…………….. which applies to you can be found in The Employee Handbook.

Exercise Five

Match the words with their definitions

Grievance   Procedure   Redundancy

Entitlement   Notice

1. A formal complaint by an employee.

   ………………………………………..

2. The established way of doing something.

   ……………………………………….

3. Time period from the day of handing in your resignation to the day that you leave.

   ………………………………………..

4. Your job is no longer required.

....

5. The right to do something.

....

Exercise Six

Match them up

There are several ways to be dismissed. Match them up.

1) Unfair dismissal   2) Wrongful dismissal

3) Constructive dismissal

a) The employee was dismissed without the employer following the notice period stipulated in the Contract of Employment.

b) The Employee was dismissed in this way when the Employer did not have a good reason for firing him or her.

c) The Employee feels that because of the harsh work environment, they were forced to resign.

1) .... 2) .... 3) ....

Genuine Occupational Requirements

The Equality Act of 2010 states that it is illegal for somebody to be treated unfairly because of a particular characteristic. However, there are some circumstances where the job would require somebody of a particular sex or race. Here are some examples:

- An black actor playing Malcom X
- A man working as an attendant in a male toilet
- Servants in private households
- A requirement for the speaker of a particular language (e.g.working in sales).

Job Advertisement

Marshall puts a job advertisement on the window of his Italian restaurant.

Marshall's Restaurant is looking for a Russian-speaking waitress aged between 19 and 29 to work evening shifts on various days each week.

Wage is £5 per hour but you get to keep any tips that the customer passes on to you.

Derek sees the advertisement, takes a photograph and posts it on his Instagram page with a caption saying 'this was my dream job and I can't apply for it.'

Which laws do you think have been broken by this advertisement?

Exercise Seven
A law graduate friend of Derek writes an email to him about his social media post. Fill in the prepositions and articles that have been omitted.

Dear Derek

I just saw your Instagram post and felt compelled 1) ….. email you 2) ……….. the job advertisement you posted earlier.

The advert breaks several laws 3) ……… discrimination and you would be 4) ……….. your rights 5) ……… take further action.

To begin 6)…….., it is unlawful 7)………. 8)……….. restaurant to post 9) ……….. advertisement for a waitress as it is sex discrimination There is no reason why 10) ……..….. man cannot do that job.

Secondly, the restaurant owner is discriminating on grounds of age 11) ….…….. he cannot stipulate that only women in their twenties are allowed to apply 12) ….……. the job.

Thirdly, the wage being offered is 13) ….……… the statutory minimum wage as tips should not be included as part of your wage.

There is one question regarding the Russian speaker. It may be possible that the restaurant has many Russian clients and so it may be useful to have a Russian speaker 14) ….……. staff but as it is an Italian restaurant in a town not known for having a Russian diaspora, I do question the owner's thought process.

I would suggest that you go to The Equality and Human Rights Commission website and fill 15) …..……... the form to complain about the advertisement. You might also be able to bring a claim against Marshall's at an Employment Tribunal if you wish.

I hope that helps.

Steven Smith

Employment Tribunals

If you feel that you have been dismissed unfairly, you can try and reach a negotiated settlement with your Employer via Acas (the Advisory Conciliation and Arbitration Service). If this attempt at conciliation fails, you can make a claim with an Employment Tribunal. The following page shows how an ET is structured.

THE EMPLOYMENT TRIBUNAL HEARING ROOM

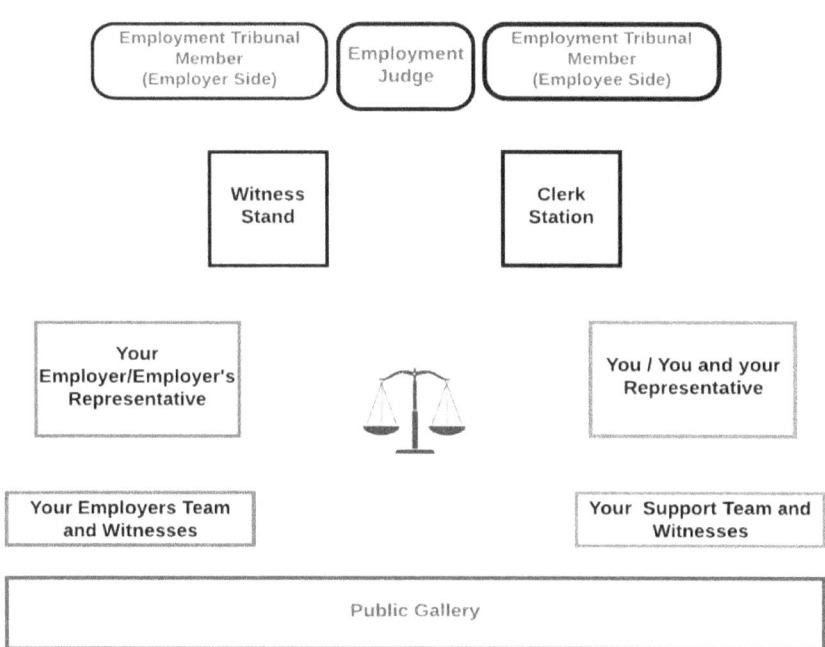

This is the layout of an Employment Tribunal. As you can see, there are representatives of employers and employees on the panel as well as a neutral employment judge.

The Tribunal can hear cases of dismissal and discrimination. The article below deals with a case of sex discrimination.

Exercise Eight
Newspaper article

Here is a newspaper article about an Employment Tribunal claim. Fill in the missing words which can be found underneath.

A female security guard who was wrongly and repeatedly called "Mr" by her 1) ……………….. has won £2,000 in compensation.

Eryl Barnaby was working as a security guard at a shopping centre in the south west of England when her 2) ………………….. repeatedly referred to her as 'Mr' on the phone and in employment records.

Being addressed as a man by her colleagues, despite being a woman, left her feeling upset and annoyed at their behaviour.

Miss Barnaby told the Kent Employment Tribunal that she was referred to as a man at least 16 times in written

3) ………………… and in telephone calls while she worked for the company.

Her 4) ………………... employer claimed that the mistakes were because of administrative errors that had now been 5) ………………..

Employment Judge James Lavelle told the court: "Miss Barnaby was called 'Mr' on 16 separate occasions in writing and 6) …………….... As the company operates in a male dominated 7) ……………..., perhaps even more attention ought to be paid to avoid discriminatory assumptions."

"Miss Barnaby clearly had increased anxiety and stress and found this extremely 8) ……………... and she was in tears on several occasions," he said.

The tribunal found her claim of harassment was well founded and awarded Miss Barnaby £4,000 for injury to feelings.

Documents   Rectified   Employer   Verbally

Colleagues   Grating   Former   Sector

Exercise Nine
Crossword

U	F	Q	W	A	G	E	U	A
N	D	A	O	P	Q	V	Y	H
I	Z	Q	W	P	A	R	T	P
O	M	T	E	R	M	S	N	F
N	B	R	R	E	S	U	M	E
P	O	R	Y	N	X	N	Y	A
S	H	I	F	T	A	F	E	R
H	A	N	D	I	N	A	W	N
D	S	K	L	C	F	I	M	U
R	A	I	S	E	T	R	J	K

1)   Person who learns a trade.

2)   Organisation that protects worker rights.

3)   The American English word for curriculum vitae.

4) Contract designed to ensure that information is kept confidential.

5) Phrasal verb meaning 'to give notice'.

6) A weekly salary.

7) ………….. dismissal.

8) An increase in salary.

9) To work many hours over four days.or so.

10) To make a living.

11) If you are not full time, you are this.

12) Parts of a contract

6. Intellectual Property Law

Intellectual Property Law

Intellectual property (IP) law remains a growing area of law and deals with the protection of inventions, designs, artwork, music and brands.

Artists and inventors need to know that others can be stopped from copying or selling their creative efforts.

Intellectual property rights can be divided into the following subject areas:

Trademarks
Patents
Designs
Copyright
Trade secrets

A patent is used to protect your invention. You can take out a patent if you have created something original which can be used by people. If someone copies your idea and sells it without your permission, you can take legal action against them. In the UK, a patent lasts for 20 years and can be renewed.

A trademark is a symbol or expression representing a company or product. The McDonald's golden arch is a great example of a symbol as a trade mark while Nike's 'just do it' slogan has also been trademarked. The mark must be distinctive in order to be registered.

In the United Kingdom, copyright protection is granted automatically when an author finishes an original work. This stops others from stealing your work. You get copyright protection by creating a film, a literary work and website content among other things.

IP lawyers specialise in either contentious or non-contentious IP law. Non-contentious work is legal work that should not go to court and includes registering trademarks and patents and drafting agreements.

Contentious work might involve a court hearing and would include areas such as copyright or patent infringement or the sale of counterfeit items.

Exercise One
Comprehension

    1. What is a patent?

        ....

        ....

2. How long does a patent last for in the UK?

……………………………………………………………………………..

3. What must a trademark be?

……………………………………………………………………………

……………………………………………………………………………..

4. What is the difference between contentious and non-contentious law?

……………………………………………………………………………….

……………………………………………………………………………….

Exercise Two
Keywords in IP Law

Passing Off   Cybersquatting   Trade secret

Design right   Fair dealing   Licence

1) "My friend has just bought the website bbc.co and is hoping to sell it to the BBC for a big profit."

....

2) "He opened a hotel called Trump Guest House and soon received an email from lawyers for the Trump Corporation."

....

3) "If you sign this, you won't be infringing on my client's rights."

....

4) "This protects the shape and configuration of something from being copied by someone else."

....

5) "He photocopied the book 20 times and started selling it to acquaintances. It's not covered by that."

....

Exercise Three

James Dyson v Hoover

Fill in the missing words:

Ruled   Infringing   Multinationals   Damages

Inventor   patent   Rights

James Dyson is the wealthiest British 1) …….....………….. so it should come as no surprise that other companies might wish to appropriate his designs.

In this recent court case, Hoover agreed to pay Dyson over £4 million for 2) ………...……………………….....….. the 3) ………………….. for Dyson's dual cyclone cleaner. The amount is believed to be one of the highest awards for 4) …………..………………. in a patent case in the UK.

The Patent Court 5) …...….....……………...... that Hoover had copied Dyson's designs when manufacturing a range of bagless vacuum cleaners.

Mr Dyson told the press: "The patent system can work. I hope it encourages inventors who have their ideas stolen by 6) .... to fight for their patent 7) ...."

Exercise Four
Comprehension Questions

1. One newspaper headline said that Hoover had been 'taken to the cleaners' in this case. What do you think this idiom means?

   ....

   ....

2. Which court heard the case?

   ....

3. What did Hoover do wrong?

....

....

....

Trademarks

A bar inspired by the Netflix television show Stranger Things received a superb letter from lawyers linked to the television streaming service.

The letter is known as a cease and desist letter and is used by lawyers to warn people of possible legal action if they do not comply with the terms of the letter.

While many of these types of letters can be scary to receive, the lawyers in this case decided to be creative. And the legal letter went viral as a result of this. Here is an extract from the letter:

"My walkie-talkie is busted so I had to write this note instead. I heard you launched a Stranger Things pop-up bar. Look, I don't want you to think I'm a total wastoid, and I love how much you guys love the show. But unless I'm living in the Upside Down, I don't think we did a deal with you for this pop-up. You're obviously creative types, so I'm sure you can appreciate that it's important to us to have a say in how our fans encounter the worlds we build.

We're not going to go full Dr. Brenner on you, but we ask that you please (1) not extend the pop-up beyond its six-week run ending in September, and (2) reach out to us for permission if you plan to do something like this again. Let me know as soon as possible that you agree to these requests.

We love our fans more than anything, but you should know the Demogorgon is not always as forgiving. So please don't make us call your mom."

The owners closed the bar.

Exercise Five
Rewrite the following informal sentences into more formal sentences.

1. Reach out to us for permission if you plan to do something like this again.

....

....

....

2. I don't think we did a deal with you for this pop-
   up.

....

....

....

3. I don't want you to think I'm a total wastoid.

....

....

4. Please don't make us call your mom.

....

....

Summarising

As a competent and compelling legal writer, you must have an ability to summarise complex laws well. Case law and statutes can be confusing for non-lawyers who may need these complicated legal matters explained to them.

How to summarise

- Read and understand the text carefully

- Ask yourself why the author wrote this text

- Identify the main points raised

- Express those key points in your own words

The Intellectual Property Act (2014) was drafted to modernise British IP law, particularly in relation to design and patents. Here is an extract from the statute:

"7B

Right of prior use

(1)

A person who, before the application date, used a registered design in good faith or made serious and effective preparations to do so may continue to use the design for the purposes for which, before that date, the person had used it or made the preparations to use it.

(2)

In subsection (1), the "application date", in relation to a registered design, means—

(a)

the date on which an application for the registration was made under section 3, or

(b)

where an application for the registration was treated as having been made by virtue of section 14(2), the date on which it was treated as having been so made.

(3)

Subsection (1) does not apply if the design which the person used, or made preparations to use, was copied from the design which was subsequently registered.

(4)

The right conferred on a person by subsection (1) does not include a right to licence another person to use the design.

(5)

Nor may the person on whom the right under subsection (1) is conferred assign the right, or transmit it on death (or in the case of a body corporate on its dissolution), unless—

(a)

the design was used, or the preparations for its use were made, in the course of a business, and

(b)

the right is assigned or transmitted with the part of the business in which the design was used or the preparations for its use were made."

(2)

This section applies only to designs registered under the Registered Designs Act 1949 after the commencement of this section.

Summarise all or part of the statute to the best of your ability. Make sure that you include an introduction, a main part and a conclusion. You will find an example below.

Section three of the Act states that subsection one no longer applies if the design was copied from something that was later registered.

Focus on using the active voice wherever possible and using strong and relevant verbs to summarise effectively. Use words such as states, sets forth, makes clear, etc.

Exercise Seven
Odd Words Out

Find and circle the odd word out in each group.

1. Pass off   Copy   Patent   Infringe

2. Trademark   Copyright   Cybersquatting   Patent

3. Grant   Award   Remove   Give

4. Liable   Responsible   Culpable   Valid

5. Disclaimer   Affirmation   Refusal   Denial

6. Unfair   Justifiable   Arbitrary   Inexcusable

Exercise Eight
Fill in the missing words

1) Intellectual Property deals with …………….………...…. assets.

2) IP Law deals with areas such as ……………………..….., trademarks and ……………………………..………...

3) If I copy somebody else's invention, I may be guilty of ………………………………………….

Exercise Nine
End User Licence Agreement

The End User Licence Agreement is a contract between the provider of software and the person who eventually uses it. This is a contract that tells the end user what they can and cannot do with the product. Below is an extract from a typical End User Licence Agreement.

Restrictions

You agree not to, and you will not permit others to:

a) license, sell, rent, lease, assign, distribute, transmit, host, outsource, disclose or otherwise commercially exploit the Application or make the Application available to any third party.

The following clause deals with severability. Fill in the missing words from the choice below.

Severability

If any 1) .... of this Agreement is held to be unenforceable or invalid, such provision will be changed and interpreted to 2) .... the objectives of such provision to the greatest 3).............................. possible under 4) .... law and the remaining provisions will continue in full force and effect.

Extent   Provision   Applicable Accomplish

Term and Termination

This 5) ……..……………... shall remain in 6)……..………..……… until 7) ………..……….. by you or Legal English UK

Legal English UK may, at its sole 8) ………….………….., at any time and for any or no reason, suspend or terminate this Agreement with or without prior notice.

This Agreement will 9) …………….…………….. immediately, without prior notice from Legal English UK, in the event that you fail to 10) ……….………... with any 11) ………….………….. of this Agreement. You may also terminate this Agreement by deleting the Application and all copies 12) ……….…………….. from your mobile device or from your desktop.

Upon termination of this Agreement, you shall cease all use of the Application and delete all copies of the Application from your mobile device or from your desktop.

Agreement Thereof   Terminated Comply

Discretion   Provision   Effect   Terminate

Exercise Ten
Passive Voice or Active Voice
The passive voice focuses attention on the person, place or thing that has experienced an action rather than who performed the action. The active voice focuses on the person who performs the action.

Where possible you should use active voice in your sentences.

Turn these statements from passive to active voice.

1) The patent was denied to the inventor by The Patent Office.

....

....

2) He was told that the right of fair dealing was not applicable in this instance.

....

....

3) The assignee was delighted to receive the rights to the patent from the assignor.

....

....

4) James Dyson was amazed when he heard that he had won £4 million in damages from Hoover.

....

....

Exercise 11
Test your legal knowledge

1) Which of the following would not be protected under UK copyright law?

a)   A film
b)   An improvised speech
c)   A musical score
d)   The design for a building

2) Should I write © to protect the copyright of something that I have written? If not, what should I do?

....

....

....

3) How many years are the following protected for?

Literary works   70 years/50 years
Films   70 years/50 years
Broadcasts   70 years/50 years

4) What does 'passing off' mean? Can you think of an example?

....

....

....

6. Tort

Tort

A tort occurs when an individual commits a wrong on another individual. Torts include nuisance, personal injury, invasion of privacy, damage to property and defamation.

Criminal cases are usually brought by the state through the Crown Prosecution Service (CPS) while civil cases are brought to The County Court by individual citizens.

In a recent case, neighbours of the Tate Modern art gallery in London complained that a new part of the building was a nuisance as visitors could look into their apartments from the balcony opposite. They lost the case with the court holding that there was no right to privacy.

In a recent trespass case, an injunction was granted to prevent YouTubers from recording stunts in a shopping centre.

The main civil law remedies are injunctions and financial damages.

Exercise One
Match the words from the article with their definitions.

Injunction   Nuisance   Damages

Damage   Trespass

1) Court Order forbidding someone from doing
   something.

....

2) Causing inconvenience or annoyance to somebody.

....

3) Financial compensation.

....

4) Physical harm to something.

....

5) Knowingly entering somebody's land without
   permission.

....

Exercise Two
Wordsearch
Find the words in the wordsearch from the clues below.

P	D	E	F	E	N	C	E	Z	W
N	E	G	L	I	G	E	N	C	E
K	F	L	I	N	J	U	R	Y	U
D	A	M	A	G	E	S	L	D	C
J	M	N	B	L	A	T	I	X	H
M	A	K	I	S	B	E	B	O	A
R	T	S	L	A	N	D	E	R	T
O	I	Q	I	H	M	U	L	X	T
J	O	F	T	O	R	T	U	E	E
D	N	L	Y	R	R	Y	L	J	L

1) Not showing a sufficient duty of care to your neighbour
2) Responsibility
3) General word for spreading lies and gossip.
4) Saying lies that will harm the reputation of somebody.
5) Writing lies that will harm the reputation of somebody
6) You have this to your neighbour.
7) You can cause this if you are irresponsible.

8) An old English word for property that is still used occasionally.
9) Another word for compensation.
10)   If you are being sued, you need a good ....
11)   What we are studying right now.

Exercise Three
Heads of Tort

There are several heads of tort. Match them to their definitions.

Negligence   Trespass to land   Defamation

Trespass to the person   Nuisance

Occupier's liability

1) Not showing sufficient duty of care.

....

2) Writing or telling a lie about someone with the intention of causing harm to their reputation.

....

3) Walking into somebody's garden without their permission.

....

4) Intentional interference with somebody

....

5) Accidents in buildings.

....

6) Causing an annoyance

....

Exercise Four
The case of Donoghue v Stevenson

Fill in the spaces in the essay about this pivotal contract law case with this selection of words.

From   omissions   At   Poured

Sued   Manufacturer   Duty Relationship

Neighbour Bought   Affected   In

One of the most well-known tort cases is Donoghue v Stevenson 1) ……….……....1932.

Mrs Donoghue visited a cafe in Paisley in Scotland with a friend. The friend 2) ……...……………………....…… her a bottle of ginger beer and some ice cream. The ginger beer was 3) ………….…….. a dark bottle so it was impossible to see inside.

As was the fashion 4) ……….…….. the time, Mrs Donoghue 5) ……….…….….. some of the ginger beer over her ice cream and a dead snail came out.

Mrs Donoghue 6) ……...……………………....…… Stevenson, the 7) …….…..……………… of the drink, for negligence.

The question was whether Stevenson owed a 8) …………….. of care to Donoghue even if he had not sold her the ginger beer. Was the 9) ………….…..………… so close that Stevenson should have foreseen that a customer would not have been able to see inside the bottle before drinking it?

While the case was heard in the Scottish courts, it eventually found its way to the House of Lords, which was then the Supreme Court of the UK. It was there that Lord Justice Atkin delivered his famous judgement regarding the 10) …………..………… principle:

"You must take reasonable care to avoid acts or 11) ……..…………. which you can reasonably foresee would be likely to injure your neighbour. Who, then, in law is my neighbour? The answer seems to be – persons who are so closely and directly affected by my act that I ought reasonably to have them in contemplation as being so affected when I am directing my mind to the acts or omissions which are called in question."

In other words, you should consider anybody who is closely or directly 12) ……..…………. by your act (or your failure to act) even if you have never met them.

Exercise Five
Answer the following questions about the case of Donoghue v Stevenson.

1. What did Mrs Donoghue's friend buy in the cafe?

   ....

2. Why couldn't Mrs Donoghue or the cafe owner see what was inside the bottle?

   ....

3. Where did this incident take place?

   ....

4. Which court finally heard the case?

   ....

5. What is the name of the court that would hear this case if it was being heard today?

   ....

Exercise Six
Collocations
A collocation is a word that partners with another word.
Try and match these words.

Award	Falsehood
Claim	Principle
Malicious	Damages
County	Injury
Owe	Liability
Neighbour	An injunction
Make	A Claim
Vicarious	A Duty
Cause	Wrong
Sustained	Court
Civil	Damage
Issue	Compensation

Exercise Seven

Now place the collocations into the sentences below using the correct tense.

1. The court …………………………… to stop John from entering his neighbour's land.

2. She claimed that she had ……………………………….. after slipping on the floor.

3. You can ………………………..………. at the ……………………………… if you feel that you have been wronged.

4. A tort is a ……………………………………………….

5. He was ………………………………...……... of £20,000.

6. The question is whether …………………….....…………. means that the employer was responsible for the actions of his employee.

Exercise Eight
Identify the tort involved in each instance.

1. Eric has been writing a string of lies about his doctor on Twitter.

   ....

2. John has been parking his car in his neighbour's driveway.

   ....

3. A neighbour keeps having parties with loud music until late at night.

   ....

4. Susan was shopping in her local supermarket when she slipped on some milk that had been spilt on the floor.

   ....

Exercise Nine
Fill in the missing prepositions in the sentences below.

1. The court found Mr Hancock liable ……….. the damages.

2. If you have had a serious accident, you may be entitled …………... compensation.

3. The law of tort imposes a duty ……. every citizen.

4. I have proof …………….. trespass as I have a CCTV camera outside my home.

5. Her client acted ………….. a negligent manner ………… my client.

6. A reasonable person would have acted differently …………. those circumstances.

7. It could not have been foreseen ……..…… the defendant.

8. This is dependent …………. the circumstances of the case.

Exercise Ten
Phrasal Verbs

A phrasal verb is formed when you join a verb and a preposition (or two) together to create an idiomatic verb. For example, *get way with* means to escape without being caught: *She got away with murder.* Join the verbs and prepositions together and fill in the sentences below.

Draw   Enter   Weigh   Get

Sum   Turn   End

And these prepositions. Some may not be required.

Up   Into   Out   From

1. They have .... negotiations over costs.

2. The jury .... the defendant and prosecution arguments.

3. If you take a case to the County Court you may .... on the losing side.

4. The claimant's solicitors were asked to ……………...… a list of items that had been taken by the defendant.

5. As he ……………………..…………….. the case, the judge sighed despondently.

Exercise 11
Grammar and word choice
Even advanced level students sometimes struggle with grammar and word choice. Look at the sentences below and correct them where necessary.

1) Before the case came to court, the client wanted to speak to her solicitor since Tuesday.

……………………………………………………………………….

……………………………………………………………………...

2) She suggested negligence but there was little prove of this.

………………………………………………………………………

……………………………………………………………………..

3) He wanted to practice as a solicitor but nobody would rent him.

....

....

4) Six months ago I have been argued my first case in The County Court.

....

....

5) By this time next week, we worked at this firm for two years.

....

....

6) If you would make the claim earlier, you would be within the limitation period.

....

Exercise 12

Circle the correct word in these sentences.

1) Donoughue v Stevenson is a landmark/terrific/precedent case in tort law.

2) As soon as the neighbour started tramping/developing/encroaching on his land, she instructed her solicitors to take the necessary steps.

3) She brought a(n) case/trial/situation against the tortoise/torthead/tortfeasor.

4) If you feel that you have been wronged, you can take legal response/action/redress.

5) I write in respect of/in the name of/on behalf of my client.

6) If you allege slander, the liability/focus/onus lies with the claimant to prove that their reputation has been damaged.

7) There are several noses/faces/heads of tort including nuisance and trespass.

What happens if a defendant can't pay?

What happens if defendants are unable to pay debts which the county and high courts have ordered to be paid? In these instances, a bailiff or enforcement agent will be obliged to recover the money.

They do this by visiting premises where the defendant is believed to live or work. Once they find them, they can ask that they pay the money owed in full or set up a payment plan. If no money is forthcoming, they can seize goods that they believe are of enough value to pay off the debt. They may also need to recover money for costs.

Debtors are given seven days' notice of a visit by the agents. They cannot force entry into somebody's home but if a door is open then they can gain peaceful entry.

Exercise 13
Comprehension Questions

1. What is the job title for the person tasked with recovering debts that have not been paid?

   ....

2. Which courts can order debt recovery?

   ....

3. What happens when you are visited by one of the officers of the court?

   ....

   ....

   ....

Answers

1) Legal Writing

Exercise One
1) As you can see from the attached document, you should leave the building immediately.
2) We write in reference to the above-named property.
3) The bias of the court may affect the outcome of the case.
4) The court decided to re-examine the controversy caused by the Netflix documentary.
5) The parties mentioned above did not know about the problems they had caused.
6) From now on, any defendant must address the court via their lawyer.
7) Please find my CV enclosed.

Exercise Two
1) The Judge believed that the claimant could not provide strong evidence.
2) The contract did not indicate that the package should have been delivered to Mark Knox.
3) The barrister disagreed with the judge.
4) Four people committed numerous acts of fraud if allegations are to be believed.
5) I suggested that they use one solicitor for everybody.
6) The other side wants to settle.

Exercise Three
Dear Mr X
Thank you for taking the time to visit our office this morning.

I am sorry to hear that you have been dismissed from your job after your employer alleged that you had been stealing stationery from the office. There appears to be no evidence of this and I am confident that we can come to a positive conclusion.

Our first action will be to write to your former employer requesting full details of the allegations. If he responds with similar unproven allegations then we can proceed to bring a claim at the Employment Tribunal.

There may also be a case for defamation of character if there is sufficient evidence. I explained that this is a costly process so you should consider whether you wish to proceed or not.

If you have any questions, please do not hesitate to contact me.

Yours sincerely

Exercise Four
1) The jury found the defendant not guilty by majority verdict.
2) I felt that the judge wanted to rule that the evidence should not be admitted.
3) We feel that compensation under £50,000 is unacceptable.
4) We proposed that our client accept the offer.
5) The judge delivered the verdict to great silence minus one or two.
6) The bailiff removed the protestor (later charged with contempt) from the courtroom.
7) The defendant murdered the victim with a shotgun.
8) Their client could have received a lighter sentence according to counsel.

Exercise Five
1) D, 2) j, 3) a, 4) k, 5) h, 6) c, 7) f, 8) i, 9) b, 10) g, 11) l, 12) e

Exercise Six
1) She argued that...

2) He chose a trainee over an associate
3) The man admitted that he had stolen the wallet
4) The translator interpreted the affidavit
5) The doctor referred the defendant to a psychiatrist
6) The parties agreed not to compete in each other's territories.

Exercise Seven
1) Chris is definitely one of the people in the video; he is tall and slim with black hair and always wears a dark jacket and blue jeans. His jeans have holes in them and his trainers are scruffy too. He usually sits at the back of the lecture hall and often seems to be asleep. However, when the exam results are given out he always gets an "A". I don't think he's as lazy as he appears to be.

2) The woman wandered into the area; she claimed to know the man in charge but he said that he had never met her before in his life (which was not what she wanted to hear) so she started shouting and screaming and punching and kicking people until the police came and arrested her. When she went to the police station her solicitor had a word with the police and told them that she was under a lot of stress so they let her off with a warning.

3) Your claim for damages is likely to be considered seriously by the court but you should note that there are mitigating factors which they may bring into consideration and which are beyond our control. Even if we had a chance to change the narrative, it is only a small chance that is unlikely to sway the court.

4) The court clerks instructed the twelve members of the jury not to speak about the case outside the courtroom. The clerks want to protect jury integrity and there were concerns about media interest in the case.

5) While the witness maintained a relaxed demeanour through the cross-examination, there was something about her

answers that didn't ring true and I felt that the jury picked up on this.

Exercise Eight

1) There is not going to be another offer until they clarify the situation.
2) The Judge asked the jury to decide if the defendant was guilty or not.
3) Government officials can accept hospitality if it complies with ethics rules.
4) You are not speaking the truth when you explain your change of mind.
5) As the investigation may be flawed, my client is taking legal advice.
6) The council issued a closure order after sending a team to look at the premises.

Exercise Nine

1) This room may be used by up to seven people.
2) Please do not attempt to contact the witness (unavoidable here).
3) My client did not commit the crime (unavoidable but can be cleared up)
4) My client's actions were entirely innocent.
5) The agreement was complex and my client's attempts at revision did not breach the contract.

2) Legal Profession
Exercise One
1) solicitor, 2) silk, 3) chambers, 4) will, 5) traineeship, 6) pupillage, 7) committed, 8) barrister

Exercise Two

1) ceiling, 2) wall, 3) jury/jury box, 4) jury box/jury, 5) clerk to the court, 6) judge, 7) wig, 8) bench, 9) witness, 10) witness box, 11) evidence, 12) barrister/counsel/QC/silk/prosecutor, 13) solicitor, 14) solicitor, 15) press box/spectator area, 16) spectator area/press box, 17) defence counsel/defence barrister/ 19) bailiff, 20) stenographer

Exercise Three
a) Responsibilities, b) separation, c) hear, d) ruling, e) appeal, f) leads

Exercise Four
1) 12, 2) October 2009, 30 House of Lords

Exercise Five
1) largest, 2) highest, 3) difficult/interesting/any appropriate adjective, 4) better/worse/sexier 5) less lenient, 6) easier

Exercise Six
Take over - take control, look over - read quickly, Serve upon - deliver, Adhere to - follow, Bail out - save, Rule out - discard,

Exercise Seven
1) Adhere to,, 2) served upon, 3) bailed out, 4) look over, 5) taken over

Exercise Eight
1) Fit and proper, 2) null and void, 3) part and parcel,

Exercise Nine
1) Miss Nash will be representing you.
2) The sale of your property is likely to take place on 30 June.
3) If you can prove your enthusiasm for the training contract then we would be delighted to welcome you to the firm.

4) The court felt that the defendant was guilty.
5) While there are nine justices on The US Supreme Court, the UK one has 12.
6) The training contract takes two years and trainees work in four different departments.

Exercise Ten

Heretofore - before, Affidavit - witness statement, Bailiff - debt collector, Stare decisis - it stands, Hereditament - property that cannot be inherited

3) COMPANY LAW

Exercise One
1. Partnership; 2) limited company, LLP, PLC' 3) limited company, PLC; 4) sole traders; 5) PLC, limited company, LLP; 6) partnership, LLP; 7) PLC; 8) limited company, LLP, PLC; 9) LLP, partnership

Exercise Two
1) Sole, 2) unlimited, 3) creditors, 4) distinguish, 5) independent

Exercise Three
1) B, 2) e, 3) a, 4) d, 5) c

Exercise Four
1) Coffee shop/retail, 2) limited liability, easy access to finance, tax incentives, 3) Potential of losing a significant amount of money.

Exercise Five
1) Liquidate, 2) acquaintance, 3) Antagonist, 4) department, 5) rights issue, 6) confederation

Exercise Six
1) Her Majesty's Customs and Excise collect taxes.
2) You are responsible personally for all the debts of the company in the event of bankruptcy.
3) Less paperwork, less administration, unlikely to take on lots of debt.

Exercise Seven
1) e, 2) a, 3) d, 4) b, 5) c

Exercise Eight
1) To; 2) at, of; 3) to, 4) between, 5) for, 6) up, 7) to

Exercise Nine
1) Incorporate, 2) dividend, 3) authorised, 4) liability, 5) sleeping

Exercise Ten
1) Comply, 2) duty of loyalty and duty of care, 3) keep a record of accounts, 4) cancelled

Exercise 11
1) Annual General Meeting and Extraordinary General Meeting
2) The Companies Act 2013
3) A vote by hand of the people in the room

Exercise 12
1) Ex-dividend, 2) index fund, 3) broker, 4) go public, 5) market maker, 6) stamp duty, 7) commission, 8) offer

Exercise 13
Research - Reconnaissance, confirm - authenticate, ship - deliver, accept - acknowledge, get - obtain, owner - principal, record - write down, mention - cite,

Exercise 14
1) Acquire, 2) debenture, 3) franchise, 4) hostile, 5) LLP, 6) split, 7) target, 8) joint, 9) asset, 10) dividend

Exercise 15
1) Sole trader for the moment as the financial risk is low, 2) LLP as less risk, 3) limited company, 4) Sole trader would be easier but a limited company is feasible.

Exercise 16
1) Memorandum of association, 2) articles of association, 3) negotiation, 4) Partnership agreement, 5) M&A law

4) CONTRACT LAW
Exercise One
1) study/learn, 2) binding, 3) offeree, 4) intention, 5) capacity, 6) counter-offer,

Exercise Two
1) Unilateral and bilateral; 2) undue influence, mistake, duress; 3) boilerplate; 4) consideration, legal capacity; 5) invitation to treat; 6) privity

Exercise Three
1) E, 2) h, 3) a, 4) c, 5) i, 6) b, 7) d, 8) j, 9) g, 10) f

Exercise Four
1) Yes, there was an offer.
2) Yes, she accepted the offer.

3) Arguably yes. Nancy is giving up her time and Sam is spending money.
4) No. The courts have ruled that an agreement between friends and lovers of this nature does not indicate intention to create legal relations.

Exercise Five
Offer: 3, 4, 6
Invitations to treat: 1, 2, 5,

Exercise Six
   1) c, 2) b, 3) b, 4) a, 5) b

Exercise Seven
   1) d, 2) g, 3) e, 4) h, 5) b, 6) a, 7) c, 8) f

Exercise Eight
   1) c, 2) e, 3) a, 4) b, 5) d

Exercise Nine
   1) Sanction, 2) hold, 3) whole, 4) consideration, 5) allow

Exercise Ten
   1) Offeree, offeror; 2) breached, redress/compensation.damages; 3) damages/financial compensation; 4) notice; 5) into; 6) seek

Exercise 11
Half of a deal: his end of the bargain
Agree: see eye-to-eye
Ill: under the weather
Develop an illness: came down with
Separate: drifted apart
Get married: tie the knot
Financial help: pick-me-up
Help out: tide her over
Assume control: Take over

Exercise 12
1) Tie the knot, 2) under the weather, 3) end/side of the bargain, 4) drifted apart and no longer see eye-to-eye, 5) pick me up and tide her over

5) EMPLOYMENT LAW

Exercise One
1) The Employment Relations Act 1999, 2) to create equality between unions and employers, 3) initiate legal proceedings, 4) a group of people negotiating for higher salary, better rights, etc.

Exercise Two

1) Negotiated settlement, 2) employment rights, 3) redress the balance, 4) minimum wage, 5) employment tribunal, 6) unfair dismissal, 7)collective bargaining,

Exercise Three
1) Collective bargaining, 2) minimum wage, 3) unfair dismissal, 4) redress the balance, 5) negotiated settlement and employment tribunal

Exercise Four
1) Entitled, 2) discounted, 3) benefits, 4) required, 5) entitled, 6) raise, 7) procedure

Exercise Five
1) Grievance, 2) procedure, 3) notice, 4) redundancy, 5) entitlement

Exercise Six
1) b, 2) a, 3) c,

Exercise Seven

1) To, 2) about, 3) of, 4) within, 5) to, 6) with, 7) for, 8) the, 9) an, 10) a, 11) as, 12) for, 13) below, 14) on, 15) in/out.

Exercise Eight
1) Employer, 2) colleagues, 3) documents, 4) former, 5) rectified, 6) verbally, 7) environment, 8) grating

Exercise Nine
1) Apprentice, 2) (trade) union, 3) resume, 4) NDA, 5) hand in, 6) wage, 7) unfair, 8) raise, 9) shift, 10) earn, 11) part, 12) terms

6) INTELLECTUAL PROPERTY LAW

Exercise One
1) A patent is used to register an invention
2) 20 years
3) Distinctive
4) Contentious law may involve court proceedings

Exercise Two
1) Cybersquatting, 2) passing off, 3) licence, 4) design right, 5) fair dealing,

Exercise Three
1) Inventor, 2) infringing, 3) patent, 4) damages, 5) ruled, 6) multinationals, 7) rights

Exercise Four
1) Taken to the cleaners means that somebody has lost a significant amount of money.
2) The Patent Court
3) They copied an idea of Dyson.

Exercise Five
1) Please contact us if you are looking to attempt something similar in the future.
2) Our records do not show any evidence of our client agreeing to this.
3) While we do not wish to discourage your entrepreneurship…

4) If we do not hear back from you, we may be forced to initiate court proceedings.

Exercise Six (example models)
The right of prior use allows a person to continue using a design before it has been registered.

Section three of the Act states that subsection one no longer applies if the design was copied from something that was later registered.

Exercise Seven
   1) Patent, 2) cybersquatting, 3) remove, 4) valid, 5) affirmation, 6) justifiable,

Exercise Eight
   1) Intangible; 2) patents, copyright; 3) patent infringement

Exercise Nine
   1) Provision, 2) accomplish, 3) extent, 4) applicable, 5) agreement, 6) effect, 7) terminated, 8) discretion, 9) terminate, 10) comply, 11) provision, 12) thereof.

Exercise Ten
   1) The Patent Office denied the patent to the inventor.
   2) The right of fair dealing is not applicable in this instance.
   3) The assignor assigned the rights to the delighted assignee
   4) Hoover paid £4 million in damages to a delighted James Dyson

Exercise 11
   1) An improvised speech.
   2) There is no need to do this. Work is automatically copyrighted once you have written it. The best way to protect yourself is to post the work to yourself with a registered post in a sealed envelope.
   3) Literary works: 70 years, Films: 70 years, Broadcasts: 50 years

4) Pretending to be another company or that the goods you are selling are from a different company. For example, putting a badge on a Motorola phone and pretending it is an iPhone.

7) TORT

Exercise One
1) Injunction, 2) nuisance, 3) damages, 4) damage, 5) trespass

Exercise Two
1) Negligence, 2) Liability, 3) Defamation, 4) Slander, 5) Libel, 6) Duty
7) Injury, 8) Chattel, 9) Damages, 10) Defence, 11) Tort

Exercise Three
1) Negligence, 2) defamation, 3) trespass to land, 4) trespass against the person, 5) occupier's liability, 6) nuisance

Exercise Four
1) From, 2) bought, 3) in, 4) at, 5) poured, 6) sued, 7) manufacturer, 8) duty, 9) relationship, 10) neighbour, 11) omissions, 12) affected

Exercise Five
1) Bottle of ginger beer, 2) It was opaque/dark, 3) A cafe in Paisley, Scotland, 4) The House of Lords, 5) The Supreme Court

Exercise Six
1) Award compensation/damages, 2) claim compensation, 3) malicious falsehood, 4) county court, 5) owe a duty (of care), 6) neighbour principle, 7) make a claim, 8) vicarious liability, 9) cause damage, 10) sustained injury, 11) civil wrong, 12) issue an injunction

Exercise Seven

1) Issued an injunction, 2) sustained (an) injury, 3) claim compensation, county court; 4) civil wrong, 5) awarded damages, 6) vicarious liability

Exercise Eight

1) defamation/libel, 2) trespass, 3) nuisance, 4) occupier's liability

Exercise Nine

1) For, 2) to, 3) on, 4) of, 5) in, toward; 6) in or under, 7) by, 8) on/upon

Exercise Ten

1) Entered into, 2) weighed up, 3) end up, 4) draw up, 5) summed up

Exercise 11

1) The client had wanted, 2) She alleged negligence but there was little proof of this, 3) nobody would hire him, 4) I argued my case, 5) we will have worked/will have been working, 6) If you had,

Exercise 12

1) Landmark, 2) encroaching, 3) case, tortfeasor; 4) action, 5) in respect of, 6) onus, 7) heads,

Exercise 13

1) Enforcement agent/bailiff, 2) County Court/High Court, 3) Asked to pay some or all of the amount owed plus expenses. If you cannot pay then they will take items away that belong to you.